CHICAGO PUBLIC LIBRARY
SULZER REGIONAL
4455 N LINCOLN
CHICAGO, IL 60625

JUV/
GV
1007
.W35
2003

SULZER

Chicago Public Library

R0179930948

Badminton in action

W9-BBJ-631

DEC 2003

SPORTS
IN ACTION

Badminton
in Action

Niki Walker & Sarah Dann

Illustrations by Katherine Kantor

Photographs by Marc Crabtree

🌱 **Crabtree Publishing Company**

www.crabtreebooks.com

Created by Bobbie Kalman

Dedicated by Katherine Kantor
To my little sister Anna - keep on soaring!

Editor-in-Chief
Bobbie Kalman

Writing team
Niki Walker
Sarah Dann

Editorial director
Niki Walker

Project editor
Rebecca Sjonger

Editors
Kathryn Smithyman
Amanda Bishop
John Crossingham

Copy editors
Molly Aloian
Laura Hysert

Art director
Robert MacGregor

Design
Margaret Amy Reiach

Production coordinator
Heather Fitzpatrick

Photo research
Laura Hysert

Special thanks to
Kevin Murphy, Paul Murphy, Phillip Murphy, Tim D'Anna, Mark
D'Anna, Amanda Durdan, Ross Durdan, Georgia Desjardins,
Drummond Munro, Michael deBelle, Alex Bruce, Caroline Cheung,
Marlon Whyte, Jeff Clapp, Niagara Falls Badminton Club, Granite Club

Consultant
Dr. Fred Coleman, USA Badminton - www.usabadminton.org
Lance Hunter, Ontario Badminton Association -
www.ontariobadminton.on.ca

Photographs
All photographs by Marc Crabtree except the following:
Raphael Sachetat - www.badmintonphoto.com: pages 4, 5, 14, 20,
21 (bottom left), 28, 30

Illustrations
All illustrations by Katherine Kantor except the following:
Bonna Rouse: front cover, chapter heading, pages 7 (top right),
9 (plastic shuttle),29 (plastic shuttle)

Crabtree Publishing Company

www.crabtreebooks.com   1-800-387-7650

PMB 16A
350 Fifth Avenue
Suite 3308
New York, NY
10118

612 Welland Avenue
St. Catharines
Ontario
Canada
L2M 5V6

73 Lime Walk
Headington
Oxford
OX3 7AD
United Kingdom

Copyright © **2003 CRABTREE PUBLISHING COMPANY**. All rights
reserved. No part of this publication may be reproduced, stored in a
retrieval system or be transmitted in any form or by any means,
electronic, mechanical, photocopying, recording, or otherwise, without
the prior written permission of Crabtree Publishing Company.

Cataloging-in-Publication Data
Walker, Niki
  Badminton in action / Niki Walker & Sarah Dann;
illustrations by Katherine Kantor; photographs by Marc Crabtree.
     p. cm. -- (The sports in action series)
Includes index.
Offers a brief introduction to the history, techniques, equipment,
and rules of badminton, including the differences between singles
and doubles play.
  ISBN 0-7787-0334-7 (RLB) -- ISBN 0-7787-0354-1 (pbk.)
  1. Badminton (Game)--Juvenile literature. [1. Badminton (Game)]
I. Dann, Sarah. II. Kantor, Katherine, ill. III. Crabtree, Marc, ill.
IV. Title. V. Series: Sports in action.
  GV1007.W35 2003
  796.345--dc21
                                                      2003001941
                                                      LP

R0179930948

CHICAGO PUBLIC LIBRARY
SULZER REGIONAL
4455 N. LINCOLN

Contents

What is badminton?

Many people think of badminton as a relaxing backyard activity, but competitive badminton is the world's fastest **racquet** sport. Players use racquets to hit a **shuttlecock**, which is also called a shuttle or bird, back and forth over a net. They try to keep the shuttle from touching the floor on their half of the **court**. Competitive badminton players have to be in great shape. They must move quickly to reach the shuttle, which can fly at speeds of up to 200 miles per hour (322 km/hr). In a typical **match**, players run more than a mile (1.6 km) to make and return shots! They must have sharp reflexes and the ability to make good decisions quickly. In a split second, they have to decide where their opponents' shots are traveling and how best to hit the shuttle back over the net.

Point, game, match

The object of badminton is to hit the shuttle so that an opponent cannot reach it in time to send it back over the net. Players score points when their opponents miss the shuttle. They compete to score points until one of them wins a **game**. Three games make up a match. Players must win two of the three games to win the match. For more about keeping score, see pages 28-29.

Singles and doubles

Badminton can be played by two or four players at a time. **Singles** badminton is played by individual opponents. In **doubles** badminton, shown right, two pairs of players compete against one another. Most of the information in this book refers to singles badminton. For more on doubles, see pages 30-31.

Badminton is a very popular international sport. More than a billion people tuned in to watch the first Olympic badminton competition in 1992!

Welcome to the court

Competitive badminton is played indoors on a wooden surface called a court. The court is divided in half by a net. Singles and doubles courts are the same length, but they are different widths. A singles court is seventeen feet (5 m) wide, whereas a doubles court is twenty feet (6 m) wide.

Serving, receiving, and rallying

The players on the right are beginning a game. Games are made up of a series of **rallies** in which players hit the shuttle back and forth over the net. Each rally begins with one player **serving** the shuttle, or putting it into play, and the other player receiving it. The first serve of a game is always from the right-hand **service box**. The server must hit the shuttle diagonally to the opponent's service box on the other side of the net. A player loses a rally by missing the shuttle or hitting it **out-of-bounds**. A player can also lose a rally by hitting the shuttle against the ceiling or net, hitting it before it crosses the net fully to his or her side, or letting the shuttle touch any part of his or her body or clothing.

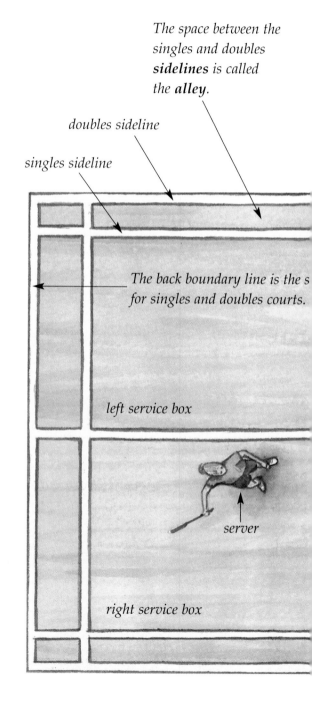

*The space between the singles and doubles **sidelines** is called the **alley**.*

doubles sideline

singles sideline

The back boundary line is the s for singles and doubles courts.

left service box

server

right service box

*In **tournaments**, an **umpire**, or judge, oversees the match. He or she keeps score and determines whether shots are out-of-bounds.*

It's a toss up

Before the first game, the players take part in a coin or shuttle toss. The winner chooses either to play on a certain **end**, or side, of the court or to serve first. The opponent then makes the other choice. For example, if the winner chooses to serve first, the opponent chooses the end at which he or she wants to play. The players switch ends at the start of every game.

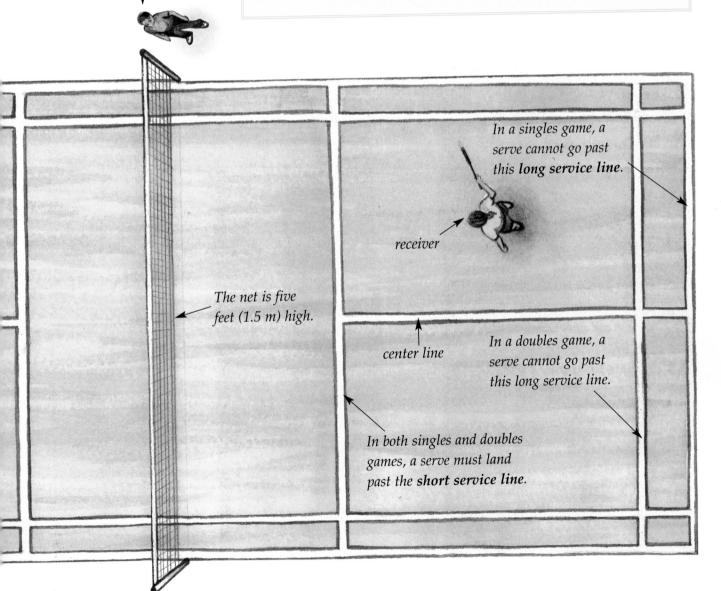

*In a singles game, a serve cannot go past this **long service line**.*

receiver

The net is five feet (1.5 m) high.

center line

In a doubles game, a serve cannot go past this long service line.

*In both singles and doubles games, a serve must land past the **short service line**.*

The essentials

You must have a racquet, shuttle, and playing area—including a net—to play badminton. You should wear comfortable clothing and proper shoes when you play. Running after the shuttle will make you hot and sweaty, so it's a good idea to bring along a towel and a bottle of water.

You'll be running and jumping a lot, so make sure your clothing is loose enough to allow you to move without getting in your way.

Wearing **court shoes** and thick socks will cushion your feet and keep you comfortable. Badminton court shoes support your feet through side-to-side, forward, and backward movements as well as quick stops. Some clubs have rules about the type of shoes you must wear on their courts. They may require you to wear shoes with light-colored soles, which don't leave marks on courts.

The racquet

Badminton racquets are lightweight, so it is easy to swing them quickly at the shuttle. Players hit the shuttle off the racquet's strings. Racquets are **weighted** differently— some are heavier at their **heads**, and others have more weight in their **grips**. Choose the racquet that feels right for you.

*The head is attached to the shaft at the **throat** of the racquet.*

*The **shaft** is long and narrow.*

A player holds the racquet by its grip.

*The head of the racquet has strings woven tightly across it. Each side of the stringed surface is called a **face**.*

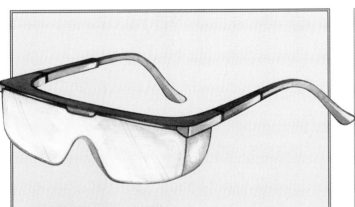

Cover your eyes

Getting hit in the eye with a racquet or shuttle can seriously injure you. To protect your eyes, wear approved safety goggles or glasses. They won't get in the way of seeing the court or the shuttle, and they'll keep your eyes safe.

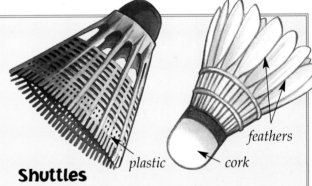

feathers

plastic   *cork*

Shuttles

There are two types of shuttles. Some are made of plastic, and others are made of feathers. Beginners and players under the age of twelve use plastic shuttles, which are slower than feather shuttles. More experienced players, as well as those in junior tournaments, use feather shuttles.

Warming up

Warming up before you practice or play helps prevent injuries. You should begin your warm-up by moving your body. Walk or jog lightly for about five minutes and then perform the stretches shown on these pages. Always stretch after you play, too, to help your muscles cool down. Doing so will keep you from getting stiff.

Lunges

Stand with your feet hip-distance apart. Take a big step forward with your left leg. When you land, position your left knee directly over your ankle. Bend your right knee so that your heel lifts off the ground. With your left leg, push yourself back to the starting position. Repeat the lunge movement with your right leg forward. Do ten lunges with each leg.

Quadriceps stretch

Stand on your right foot and lift up your left foot behind you until you can grab it with your left hand. Keep your knees together. You will feel a stretch in the front of your left leg. Hold the stretch for a count of ten and then switch legs.

Hamstrings stretch

Stand with your legs hip-distance apart. Bend your left knee so that you squat slightly. Extend your right leg in front of you, keeping your heel on the floor. Place your hands on your bent knee for balance. Flex your right foot. You should feel the stretch at the back of your leg. Hold for ten seconds and then stretch your left leg.

Calf stretch

Stand with your feet hip-distance apart. Take a big step with one leg, keeping the other foot planted. Bend the knee of your front leg so that it's directly above your ankle. Place your hands on the thigh of your front leg for support. Keep the heel of your back foot on the floor and lean your upper body forward. You should feel the stretch in the calf muscle of your back leg. Hold this position for ten seconds. Repeat with the other leg.

Rotator cuff warm-up

Hold your arms straight out to the sides so that your body forms a "T." The palms of your hands should face the ground. From the shoulders, slowly rotate your arms until your palms face upward. Slowly rotate your arms back to the starting position. Repeat ten times.

Stop signs

Reach your left arm straight out in front of you, as if you're motioning for someone to stop. Next, reach your right arm over your left arm. With your right hand, gently pull back the fingers of your left hand until you feel a stretch in your wrist. Do five stretches for each wrist.

Fancy footwork

Badminton is a fast-moving game, so you need to be quick on your feet. You'll have to move forward, backward, and side-to-side quickly without losing your balance. One of the most important skills to practice is **footwork**. Footwork is the way you move your feet to get around the court. Great footwork helps you reach the shuttle in time to position your body for making a shot. It also allows you to return to your **home base** quickly after making the shot. Your home base is the area where you feel comfortable standing between shots. From there, you can easily move to all other parts of the court.

Be ready

The **ready position** helps you stay alert and ready to spring into action. Keep your knees bent and your feet about shoulder-width apart. If you are a right-handed player, your left foot should be about half a step ahead of your right foot. Keep the racquet head high so you are ready to swing when the shuttle comes over the net. You'll stand in the ready position when receiving a serve. Between shots, you may not have time to return to the ready position, but you should always try to keep your racquet up and your feet ready for action.

This player is right-handed. The instructions given in this book are for right-handed players. If you play with your racquet in your left hand, switch the words "left" and "right" in the instructions.

Smooth moves

Footwork involves using certain steps that get you across the court fast. These steps allow you to move without needing to take your eyes off the shuttle. **Side stepping** moves you from one side of the court to the other, and **shuffle steps** are good for moving backward.

Side step

1. Start from a ready position. Slide your right foot over so it is directly beside your left foot.

2. When your right foot touches your left foot, hop to the side with your left foot.

3. Slide your right foot over again. Practice until you can cross the court with three steps.

Shuffle step

1. Start from a ready position. Move your right foot behind you. Step back lightly with your left foot.

2. As soon as your left foot touches the ground, hop backward with your right foot.

3. Step back lightly with your left foot. Practice until you can get from the net to the back of the court in three steps.

Forehand and back

Badminton requires **strategy**, or planning and decision-making. You don't have long to plan, however! During rallies, you'll have only split seconds to decide how and where to hit the shuttle. One of the first decisions you must make is whether to hit the shuttle with a **forehand** or **backhand stroke**.

The stroke, or swing, you use depends on where the shuttle is in relation to your body. When the shuttle is on the same side as your racquet hand, hit it with a forehand stroke. When the shuttle travels to the other side of your body, reach your racquet across and use a backhand stroke.

Find your grip

A grip isn't just the part of a racquet that you hold. A grip is also the way you hold your racquet. Grips are different for forehand and backhand strokes.

Nice to meet you

To find the proper grip for a forehand stroke, start by holding the shaft of the racquet in your non-playing hand. With your playing hand, "shake hands" with the racquet's grip. Wrap your fingers around the grip so that your palm is along the back of it. Your **forefinger**, or first finger, should be one inch (2.5 cm) further up the shaft than your thumb.

Backhand grip

To find the correct backhand grip, start by holding your racquet with a forehand grip. With your free hand, grab the shaft and turn the racquet. Stop when the knuckle of your playing hand's forefinger is on the top edge of the racquet's grip. Your thumb should be on the back of the racquet's grip. This thumb position gives your shot power.

forehand grip

backhand grip

During a rally, you will have to switch grips quickly to make different shots. Practice going from a forehand grip to a backhand grip until you can do it without even thinking about it.

To test whether your forehand grip is correct, stand with your racquet in front of a wall. You should be able to hold the racquet face flat against the wall. If you can't, adjust your grip and try again.

Serve it up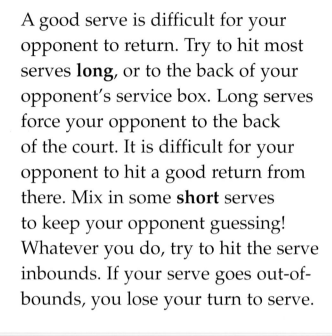

Being able to serve well can make it easier for you to score. You usually won't win a point with a serve, but a strong serve helps you gain control of a rally right from the start.

A good serve is difficult for your opponent to return. Try to hit most serves **long**, or to the back of your opponent's service box. Long serves force your opponent to the back of the court. It is difficult for your opponent to hit a good return from there. Mix in some **short** serves to keep your opponent guessing! Whatever you do, try to hit the serve inbounds. If your serve goes out-of-bounds, you lose your turn to serve.

Swing low

There are rules about how you can hit the shuttle when serving. The head of your racquet must be below your hand and the shuttle must be below your waist when you hit the serve. Most beginners hit forehand serves. More advanced players hit backhand serves, as shown left.

At first, you may find yourself watching the shuttle as you serve it. It is better to keep your eye on your target, however. Practice hitting the shuttle in the same position over and over again, until you can swing and hit it without having to look at it.

Forehand serve

1. Hold your racquet using a forehand grip. Stand facing the sideline with your feet spread slightly. Angle your front foot in the direction you want to send the shuttle. Hold the shuttle just in front of you. Drop the shuttle and swing your racquet forward to hit it in midair.

2. Twist your body as you swing the racquet using an **underhand** stroke, or one that swings the racquet toward the floor and then up. The shuttle should be in front of you and a bit to your right when you hit it.

3. Your back heel will lift as you **follow through,** or continue the swing after you hit the shuttle. Finish the stroke with your racquet high.

Ready to rally

Once the shuttle is in play, you must **cover** the entire court, or be able to reach the shuttle and hit it no matter where it goes. The better you are at covering the court, the fewer chances your opponent will have to beat you. You also have to think about winning the rally. Aim your shots at open spots on your opponent's court, so that he or she has to run in order to return them. This strategy will tire your opponent and give you chances to win the rally. Not every shot you make will be a chance to win, however. Some shots are **defensive**. They are meant to keep your opponent from scoring against you. Others set up the chance to win with your next shot. No matter what kind of shot you make, always keep your eye on the shuttle! You can read more about the different types of shots and when to use them on pages 20-27.

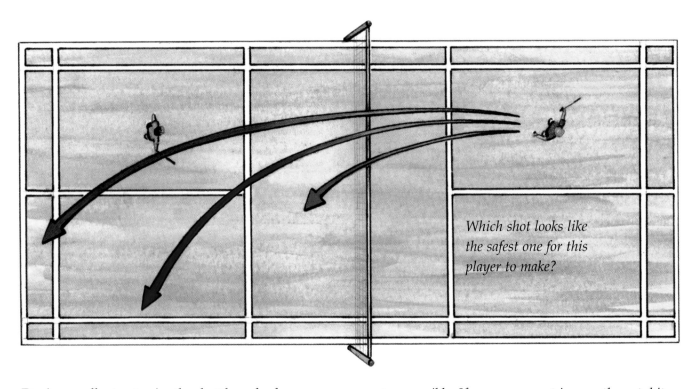

Which shot looks like the safest one for this player to make?

*During a rally, try to aim the shuttle as far from your opponent as possible. If your opponent is near the net, hit the shuttle to the back of the court, or the **backcourt** (green). If your opponent is in the backcourt, hit a shot just over the net (blue). If your opponent is near one side, aim your shot at the opposite side of the court (red).*

Keep it up

A great way to practice controlling the shuttle is to hit it up in the air over and over again. Keep your racquet face flat so that you send the shuttle straight up. Hit it lightly at first, so you don't send it too high. See how many times you can hit the shuttle without letting it fall and then try to beat your record.

Hit the wall

Hitting a shuttle against a wall is a good way to practice making returns. Try not to let the shuttle hit the floor. It will drop quickly after hitting the wall, so you have to be quick! For an added challenge, switch between forehand and backhand strokes.

Once you're good at keeping the shuttle in the air, try hitting it high up and away from yourself. Use your footwork to reach the shuttle before it hits the ground. You can also try walking as you hit the shuttle. How many times can you hit it in a row?

Scoop it up

Sometimes the shuttle will be near the floor by the time you get to it. To practice returning these shots, place a shuttle on the court and pretend that you are rushing to hit it. In one swift motion, get your racquet under the shuttle and scoop it up with a flick of your wrist. Practice until you can scoop the shuttle quickly and easily.

net shots

Net shots are shots that land close to the net. They are also called short shots. Use these shots when your opponent is at the back of the court or standing to one side of it. Two net shots are the **hairpin** and the **cross-court** net shot. The hairpin pops the shuttle over the net in a tight arc. The cross-court send the shuttle diagonally from one end of the net to the other. Since you don't want these shots to travel far, don't use much swing or follow-through. Hold your arm out straight and gently flick your wrist as you hit the shuttle.

Returning net shots

There will be times during rallies when you are on the receiving end of a short shot. You must lunge to try to return it. A lunge is a long forward step that helps you get your racquet under the shuttle before it hits the floor. You bring your back knee almost to the floor so that you can get low without losing your balance. Being able to lunge quickly and with control can keep you from losing rallies!

forehand lunge

The block

Sometimes you'll be able to guess where the shuttle is going to cross the net. If you can get to the net in time, use a **block shot** to stop the shuttle in its path. The shuttle will drop down quickly on your opponent's side. Remember that you are not allowed to reach over the net to hit the shuttle.

Practice returning short shots with forehand and backhand strokes. Don't swing your racquet—simply reach out and tap the shuttle. Don't follow through.

backhand lunge

Lifts

Lifts are great shots to use when your opponent is close to the net. A lift sends the shuttle over your opponent's head to the back of the court, so your opponent has to run after it. You can hit forehand or backhand lifts. Both are underhand shots. Lifts are also known as **underhand clears** and **lobs** because players hit the shuttle clear to the back of the court.

Forehand lifts

The way you hit forehand lifts is similar to the way you hit serves, but you hit the shuttle as it flies toward you. You need to keep your eye on the shuttle as you move your feet and racquet into a good position to hit it. Hit the shuttle when it is in front and to the right of you at about waist height. **Open**, or turn up, your racquet face slightly. The position of the shuttle and your racquet when they connect is the **point of contact**.

*When a player hits a lift that flies straight ahead, the shot is described as **down the line**. When the shuttle travels diagonally across the court, the shot is called cross court.*

Good timing

Hitting the shuttle at the proper point of contact gives you the most control. The shuttle flies across the court in a high arc. Your opponent cannot reach the shuttle before it is at the back of the court, where it drops quickly. To practice forehand lifts, ask a friend to hit or toss a shuttle to you. Try to time your swing so you hit the shuttle at the proper point of contact.

*Hit the shuttle when it is in front and to the right of you, between knee and waist height. At the point of contact, your racquet's face should be **flat**, or parallel to the net, and the back of your wrist should be facing up.*

Backhand lifts

The key to hitting a good backhand lift is to hold your racquet **back**, or pointing away from the net. Point your feet and racquet shoulder in the direction you want to send the shuttle. Keep your eye on the shuttle and swing your racquet forward to hit it. Follow through completely. At the end of your stroke, your racquet should be pointing at the net and your arms should be wide open.

Overheads

Overheads are shots you hit with your racquet raised above your head. They are powerful shots because you use the strength of both your back and your shoulders to swing the racquet. There are a few types of overhead shots—**clears**, **drops**, and **smashes**. Each one makes the shuttle travel differently over the net. You can read more about each shot on pages 25-27.

The setup

Each overhead shot has a different point of contact, but they all start with the same **preparation**, or setup. Stand facing the sideline with your feet shoulder-width apart and your knees bent. With a forehand grip, hold your racquet upright and behind your head. The head of your racquet rests on your back, and the elbow of your racquet arm points at the ceiling. With your non-racquet hand, point at the shuttle and get ready to swing your racquet.

Keep them guessing!

Because overheads all have the same preparation, it is difficult for your opponent to know whether you're going to hit a clear, a drop, or a smash. If your opponent makes the wrong guess, you can score by aiming your overhead for an open spot on the court.

To hit an overhead properly, it is very important to get right under the shuttle. You need to move quickly to get into the proper position.

Overhead clears

Like lifts, overhead clears send the shuttle to the back of your opponent's court, but clears don't arc as high as lifts do. They are useful when your opponent is near the net and you are in a difficult position on your court. While your opponent scrambles to the back of the court to return a clear, you have a bit of time to move into a better position to cover your court.

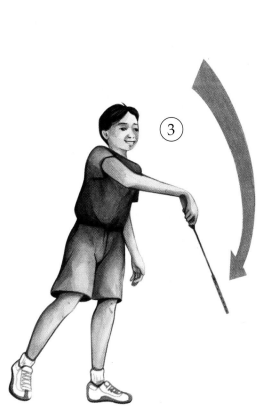

1. Move quickly into position under the shuttle as it comes down toward you. Bend your racquet arm so that the elbow points to the ceiling and the head of your racquet points to the floor.

2. Wait until the shuttle is slightly behind you and just within reach above your head before you swing your racquet up to hit it. Try to hit the shuttle when it is as high above you as you can reach.

3. Your body will twist as you swing. After you make contact with the shuttle, follow through until your arm is across your body. Make sure your follow-through is smooth and not too fast.

Drop shots

When your opponent is near the back of the court, you can use a drop shot to try to end a rally. This shot sends the shuttle just over the net, where it drops suddenly. If your opponent can't reach the shot in time, you win the rally. Even when drop shots don't win rallies, they are useful because they tire out your opponent. Try not to use them too often, however, since they work best when you catch your opponent off guard.

Fake!

To take your opponent by surprise, disguise your drop shot as an overhead clear. The drop shot starts the same way as the overhead clear—you make contact with the shuttle when it is just behind your head and as high as you can reach. As soon as you make contact, however, you **break**, or bend your wrist and barely follow through on the shot. Breaking takes the power out of the shot, so the shuttle barely makes it over the net before falling quickly. Developing the right touch for a drop shot takes a lot of practice!

The drop shot uses almost no follow-through, which takes some of the power out of the shot so the shuttle doesn't travel far. Gently bending your wrist as you hit the shuttle sends the shuttle downward.

The smash

Of all the shots in badminton, the smash is the fastest and most powerful. It sends the shuttle streaking toward the floor at a sharp angle. The smash is a good bet for hitting a **winner**, or a shot that ends a rally, because it's nearly impossible for your opponent to return it.

Reach for it

You can't be too far back in the court when you hit a smash, or the shuttle won't clear the net. The best time to hit a smash is when you are halfway between the back of the court and the net, and your opponent hits a clear that you can reach. Position yourself to hit the shuttle when it is just ahead of you and as high as you can reach. The proper point of contact is in front of your body, with your racquet swinging downward.

For a smash, swing your racquet as fast as you can. The faster your racquet is moving when it hits the shuttle, the faster the shuttle will travel.

Keeping score

Players score points only when they are serving. Servers continue to serve until they lose a rally. When receivers win a rally, they don't win a point, but it becomes their turn to serve. They then have a chance to score. Scoring is different for women's and men's badminton. Women's games go to eleven points, but if a game is tied 10-10, the first player to get ten points decides whether to **set**. If the player chooses to set, the game goes to thirteen points. If the player chooses not to set, the first to reach eleven points wins. Men's games go to fifteen points. If the score of a men's game is tied 14-14, however, the player who scored fourteen points first decides whether to set the game to seventeen points or play to fifteen points.

	I	II	III
J. ORTIZ	7	15	4
P. JONES	15	10	2

Reading the scoreboard

Many competitions use small flip scoreboards, such as the one shown right. A person flips the number cards each time the score changes. The board is set up beside the court to help the players keep track of their game. Larger scoreboards, such as the one above, are used mainly in professional tournaments. They show the score of the current game as well as games that have already been played. The scoreboard above shows that Ortiz and Jones have finished the first two games of their match. Jones won the first game with a score of 15-7. Ortiz beat Jones 15-10 in the second game, and he is winning the third game 4-2.

Before each serve, an official calls out the score. The server's score is stated first.

Team 1 | Team 2

3 | 0

Double the fun

In doubles badminton, two players called **partners** work as a team to cover their court and win points. Partners must practice moving around the court so that they cover it without getting in each other's way. Sometimes it is useful for one partner to cover the front half of the court while the other covers the back half. Teams often use this plan if their opponents hit a lot of net shots. Partners can also divide the court into a left and right half. Each partner covers the net and the back of the court on one side.

Serving and receiving

As in singles badminton, only the serving team scores points when it wins a rally. Partners take turns serving. Only one player on the receiving team can return the serve. This player stands in the receiving service box. Once this player returns the serve, the partners can move anywhere on the court.

They position themselves based on whether they are trying to score or trying to keep their opponents from scoring. When attacking, partners play front and back. The partner at the back moves forward to hit smashes, and the partner in front returns drop shots. When defending, partners often divide the court into left and right halves.

Partners on the serving team switch sides after each point. Partners on the receiving team do not change sides.

Glossary

Note: Boldfaced words that are defined in the book may not appear in the glossary.

backhand Describing a racquet position with the racquet held in front of the body

court The rectangular surface on which badminton is played

doubles Describing a match played between two teams of two players

follow through To continue a swing after the racquet has hit the shuttle

forehand Describing a racquet position with the racquet held away from the body

grip (1) the handle of a racquet; (2) the way in which the racquet is held

match A set of three badminton games

out-of-bounds Describing the area outside the court lines

point of contact The position of the racquet and the shuttle when they connect

rally A series of shots hit back and forth by players until one scores a point

ready position The position which a player holds while waiting for the shuttle

serve To begin play by first hitting the shuttle over the net

service box The area on the court from which a player serves

set To play a game until the score reaches a number decided before play

shuttlecock A name for the object hit back and forth over the net

singles Describing a match played between two people

tournament A badminton competition

Index

1 2 3 4 5 6 7 8 9 0 Printed in the U.S.A. 2 1 0 9 8 7 6 5 4 3